30

A 30-DAY DEVOTIONAL TREASURY

CHARLES FINNEY

Spiritual Power

COMPILED AND EDITED BY

LANCE WUBBELS

Emerald
Books

P.O. Box 635
Lynnwood, WA 98046

Emerald Books are distributed through YWAM Publishing. For a full list of titles, including other devotionals and classics, visit our website at www.ywampublishing.com or call 1-800-922-2143.

30-Day Devotional Treasuries Series

❀❀❀

Charles Finney on Spiritual Power
George Müller on Faith
Andrew Murray on Holiness
Charles Spurgeon on Prayer
Hudson Taylor on Spiritual Secrets
R. A. Torrey on the Holy Spirit

Introduction

The story of Charles Grandison Finney (1792–1875) can be recounted in one word: *revivals.* This is the key that unlocks the treasures of his marvelous life. Students of revival agree that Finney spearheaded one of America's greatest revivals and influenced the course of history. Everywhere he went, spiritual life burst into flame and touched whole communities for the gospel. Church rolls swelled in the wake of Finney's revivals. He is often directly or indirectly credited with the conversions of around 500,000 people.

Lawyer, college professor, pastor, and evangelist, Charles Finney left behind a record of a half-century of revival that is unparalleled in America and gave birth to a new evangelistic movement that is still employed today. He gave his life to promote "The return to and practice of biblical Christianity in the power of the Holy Spirit for the sake of God's kingdom and glory." The distinctive truths that Finney preached brought such a deep conviction of sin and such a transformation of lives that today's church does well when it studies his position on the role of the Holy Spirit in believers' lives.

Finney's own remarkable encounter with the Holy Spirit, after a deep repentance from sin, came in this fashion: "The Holy Ghost descended on me in a manner that seemed to go through me, body and soul. I could feel the impression, like a wave of electricity, going through and through me. Indeed it seemed to come in waves and waves of liquid love; for I could not express it in any other way. It seemed like the very breath of God." Shortly after this experience, Finney entered into his evangelistic ministry.

Power from on High

*All of them were filled with the Holy
Spirit and began to speak in other tongues
as the Spirit enabled them.*
—ACTS 2:4

The apostles and brethren received a powerful baptism of the Holy Spirit on the Day of Pentecost, a vast increase of divine illumination. This baptism imparted a great diversity of gifts that were used for the accomplishment of their work. It manifested itself in the following ways: The power of a holy life. The power of a self-sacrificing life. The power of a cross-bearing life. The power of great meekness, which this baptism enabled them everywhere to exhibit. The power of loving enthusiasm in proclaiming the gospel. The power of teaching. The power of a loving and living faith. The gift of tongues. An increase of power to work miracles. The gift of inspiration, or the revelation of many truths before unrecognized by them. The power of moral courage to proclaim the gospel and do the work of Christ, whatever it cost them.

Laying themselves and their all upon the altar, they besieged the throne of grace.

In their circumstances all these endowments were essential to their success; but neither separately nor all together did they constitute that power from on high that Christ promised, and that they manifestly received. That which they received as the supreme, crowning, and all-important means of success was the power to prevail with both God and man, the power to fasten *saving impressions* upon the minds of men. This last was undoubtedly the thing that they understood Christ to promise. He had commissioned the church to convert the world to Him. All that I have named above were only means, which could never secure the end unless they were vitalized and made effectual by the power of God. The apostles understood this; and, laying themselves and their all upon the altar, they besieged the throne of grace in the spirit of entire consecration to their work.

They did, in fact, receive the gifts mentioned above; but supremely and principally this power to savingly impress men. It was manifested immediately as they began to address the multitude, and three thousand were converted. God was speaking in and through them. It was a power from on high to savingly impress others.

―――∞∞∞―――

Lord Jesus, the disciples understood the meaning of Your divine promise of the Spirit. Open my eyes to understand it today. I desire the same baptism they received on the day of Pentecost, and nothing less, because of Your Word. Amen.

The Father's Promise

———∞∞∞———

"I am going to send you what my Father
has promised; but stay in the city until you have
been clothed with power from on high."
—LUKE 24:49

The disciples had been converted to Christ, and their faith had been confirmed by His resurrection. But one's conversion should not be confused with a consecration to the great work of the world's conversion. In conversion the soul deals directly and personally with Christ. The soul yields its prejudices, antagonisms, self-righteousness, unbelief, selfishness; accepts, trusts, and supremely loves Christ. All this the disciples had done. But they had received no definite commission, and no particular empowerment to fulfill a commission.

When Christ had dispelled their great bewilderment resulting from His crucifixion and confirmed their faith by repeated discussions with them, He gave them their great commission to win all nations to Himself. But He admonished them to wait at Jerusalem until they were endued with power from on high. Now observe that they assembled the men and women for prayer. They accepted their commission and undoubtedly came to understand the *nature* of the commission and the necessity of the spiritual power that Christ had promised. Continuing day after day in prayer and conference, they came to appreciate the difficulties that would beset them and to feel more and more their inadequacy to the task. It is clear that they consecrated themselves, with all they had, to the conversion of the world as their lifework. They renounced utterly the idea of living to themselves in any form, devoting themselves with all their powers to the

This dying to all that the world could offer them must have preceded their intelligent seeking of the promised empowerment.

work set before them. This self-renunciation, this dying to all that the world could offer them, must have preceded their intelligent seeking of the promised empowerment. They continued in prayer for the baptism of the Spirit, which included all that was essential to their success.

How did they wait? Not in listlessness and inactivity; not in making preparations by study and otherwise to get along without it; not by going about their business and offering an occasional prayer; but they *continued* in prayer until the answer came. They understood that Christ was to give them a baptism in the Holy Spirit. They prayed in faith. They held on, with the firmest expectation, until the power came.

———ᴏᴇᴏ———

Father, I'm willing to wait upon You for the fullness of the Holy Spirit. Prepare my heart as You did Your first disciples. My faith is fixed on You. Amen.

The Believer's Commission

———— ◦●●◦ ————

*"Whoever believes in me, as the
Scripture has said, streams of living water
will flow from within him."*
—JOHN 7:38

We, as Christians, have the same commission to fulfill as did the believers in Acts. We also have the same promise of power. It is of utmost importance that all Christians understand that this commission to convert the world is given to them by Christ individually.

Every believer has the responsibility to win as many souls as possible to Christ. This is the great privilege and duty of all Christ's disciples. There are a great many departments in this work—whether we preach, pray, write, run a business, take care of children, or administer a government office. But in every

calling, we may and ought to possess spiritual power—whatever we do, our whole life and influence should be permeated with this power to impress the truth of Christ upon men's hearts.

The first great need of the church is the realizing conviction that this commission to convert the world is given to every believer as his life-work, not just to ministers. The second need is the realizing conviction of the necessity of spiritual empowerment. Far too many believers suppose it belongs to those who are called to preach. They fail to realize that all are called to preach the gospel, that the believer's whole life is to be a proclamation of the good news. A third need is an earnest faith in the promise of the empowerment. Many believers seem to doubt whether this promise is to the whole church and to every believer. Consequently, they have no faith to lay hold of it. A fourth need is that persistence in waiting upon God for it that is commanded in the Scriptures. They give up before they have prevailed and are left to satisfy themselves with a hope of eternal life for themselves. They don't get ready to accept the great commission to work for the salvation of others and have practically lost sight of the necessity of spiritual power. Much is said of our dependence upon the Holy Spirit, but how little is this dependence realized.

The pastoral ministry is weak because the church is weak. And the church is kept weak by the weakness of the ministry. Oh for a conviction of the necessity of this empowerment of power and faith in the promise of Christ!

Father, how often has my desire for spiritual power been for myself rather than for Your glory. Break down what is selfish in me, and use me for the salvation of others. Amen.

Is It a Hard Saying?

———— ∞ ————

*"Do not leave Jerusalem, but wait
for the gift my Father promised, which
you have heard me speak about."*
—ACTS 1:4

I have said that lack of the endowment of power
from on high should be considered a disqualifica-
tion for a pastor, a deacon or elder, a Sunday-school
teacher, a professor in a Christian college, and especially for a professor in a theological seminary. Is this
a hard saying? Is it unjust, unreasonable, unscriptural?
Suppose one of the apostles, or those present on the
day of Pentecost, had failed, through apathy, selfishness, unbelief, indolence, or ignorance, to receive this
spiritual empowerment, would it have been unjust

or unreasonable to have accounted him disqualified for the work of Christ's appointment?

Christ had expressly informed them that without this empowerment they could do nothing. They were not to attempt it in their own strength, but to remain in Jerusalem until they had received it. They evidently understood Him to mean that they were to have a sense of constant waiting upon Him in prayer and supplication for the blessing. Now, suppose one of them had stayed away and attended to his own business, choosing to believe that God in His sovereignty would confer this power on them apart from waiting. He of course would have been disqualified from the work that Christ had set before them.

It was with the early church, as it should be with us, a question of faith in a promise.

And is it not true of all to whom the command to disciple the nations is given, and to whom the promise of this power is made, if through any shortcoming or fault of theirs they fail to obtain this gift? Are they not disqualified for leadership in the church?

Are they qualified to teach others to do Christ's work? Shall the church be burdened with teachers and leaders who lack this fundamental gift? The manifest apathy, indolence, ignorance, and unbelief that exist upon this subject are both amazing and inexcusable. With such a command ringing in our ears; with such an injunction to wait in constant prayer till we receive the power; with such a promise, made by such a Savior, held out to us of all the help we need from Christ Himself; what excuse can we offer for being powerless in this great work? It was with the early church, as it should be with us, a question of *faith* in a *promise*. There is a need of a great reformation in the church on this particular point.

Lord Jesus, Your promise of spiritual power is absolutely clear. So why is my faith so unsure? Search me and know my heart until faith rises to receive Your fullness. Amen.

Freedom from Sin

---

*For sin shall not be your master, because you
are not under law, but under grace.*
—ROMANS 6:14

Throughout my ministry I have found many
believers in the miserable state of the bondage
described in Romans 7—to the world, the flesh, or
the devil. It is a life of sinning, then resolving to
reform, then falling again. What is particularly sad-
dening is that many ministers give perfectly false
instruction upon the subject of how to overcome sin.
Their advice goes like this: "Name your sins, resolve
to abstain from them, and fight against them until
you overcome them. Set your will firmly against a

relapse in sin, pray and struggle, and persist until you form the habit of obedience and break all your sinful habits." While it is usually added that the believer must not depend upon his own strength, but pray for God's help, the fact is that they teach sanctification by works, and not by faith.

To eradicate selfishness from the heart by resolution is an absurdity.

All such advice is worse than useless, and often results in delusion. It has lost sight of both what really constitutes sin and of the only practical way to avoid it. In this way the outward act or habit may be overcome and avoided, while that which really constitutes the sin is left untouched. Sin is not an involuntary feeling or desire; it is a voluntary act or state of mind. Sin is that voluntary, ultimate preference or state of committal to self-pleasing out of which the volitions, the outward actions, purposes, intentions, and all the things that are commonly called sin proceed. We may suppress this or that expression or manifestation of selfishness by resolving not to do this or that, and praying and struggling against it. We may resolve upon an outward obedience, and work ourselves up to the letter of an obedience to God's commandments. But to eradicate selfishness from the heart by resolution is an absurdity. Should we cloister ourselves away in a cell and crucify all our desires, so far as their indulgence is concerned, we have only avoided certain forms of sin; but the root that really constitutes sin is not touched. All our battling with sin and desires in the outward life, by the force of resolution, only ends in making us whited sepulchers and delusional, for we cannot love God with all our heart in this manner.

———⊕———

Father, I know all too well about the bondage to sin that is described in Romans 7. How many times have I failed in the strength of my own will. I come to You that by Your power I might be free to love You with all my heart and soul. Amen.

The Role of Faith

———— ❧ ————

It is because of him that you are in Christ Jesus,
who has become for us wisdom from God—that is,
our righteousness, holiness and redemption.
—1 CORINTHIANS 1:30

All self-efforts to overcome sin are utterly futile and unscriptural. Believers are said to have "purified their hearts by faith" (Acts 15:9). Acts 16:18 affirms that saints are sanctified by faith in Christ. Romans 9:31–32 affirms that the Jews did not attain righteousness "because they pursued it not by faith but as if it were by works." The biblical doctrine is that Christ saves His people from sin through faith; that Christ's Spirit is received by faith to dwell in the heart. It is faith that works by love. Love is wrought

22

and sustained by faith. By faith believers overcome the world, the flesh, and the devil; quench the fiery darts of the enemy; and keep the flesh and carnal desires subdued. By faith we fight the good fight, not by resolution. It is simply by faith that we receive the Spirit of Christ to work in us to will and to do God's good pleasure. He sheds abroad His own love in our hearts, and thereby enkindles ours. Only the life and energy of the Spirit of Christ within us can save us from sin, and trust is the universal condition of its working within us.

One of the hardest lessons for the human heart is to renounce self-dependence and trust wholly in Christ.

How long shall this fact be mistaught? How deeply rooted in the heart of man is self-righteousness and self-dependence? So deeply that one of the hardest lessons for the human heart is to renounce self-dependence and trust wholly in Christ. When we open the door by implicit trust, He enters and takes up His dwelling with us and in us. By shedding abroad His love He quickens our whole souls into sympathy with Himself and purifies our hearts through faith. He sustains our will in the attitude of devotion. He quickens and regulates our affections, desires, appetites, and passions, and becomes our sanctification.

The Bible teaches that by trusting in Christ we receive an inward influence that stimulates and directs our activity; that by faith we receive His purifying influence into the very center of our being; that through and by His truth revealed directly to the soul He gives life to our whole inward being into the attitude of loving obedience; and this is the way, and the only practical way, to overcome sin.

Lord Jesus, I gaze upon You by faith, and I believe that You are truly my sanctification and holiness. I believe You purify my heart by faith, and You break every bondage of sin. I take those words and cling to them, as I cling to you as my Savior. Amen.

Why Spiritual Power Is Needed

———— ⟨❦⟩ ————

LORD, I have heard of your fame;
I stand in awe of your deeds, O LORD. Renew
them in our day, in our time make them
known; in wrath remember mercy.
—HABAKKUK 3:2

Habakkuk's prophecy was uttered in anticipation of the Babylonian captivity. Looking at the judgments that were coming upon his nation, the agonized prophet cried out for the Lord to use the judgments to renew His work in the midst of these awful years.

Religion is the work of man. It is something for man to do. It consists in obeying and loving God with and from the heart. It is man's duty. It is true, God influences him by His Spirit, because of man's great wickedness and reluctance to obey. If it were not necessary for God to influence men, if men were disposed to obey God, there would be no reason for this prayer. The necessity for such a prayer is that unless God interposes the influence of His Spirit, not a man on earth will ever obey the commands of God.

Unless God interposes the influence of His Spirit, not a man on earth will ever obey the commands of God.

The history of the Jews and of the church shows that there is so little firmness and stability of purpose, that unless power from on high is operating in the lives of believers, worldliness will prevail and men will not obey God. The church that is so easily swept away in the vortex of luxury, idolatry, and pride, as it is today, must cry out to God that He might renew His work by the Holy Spirit.

The Holy Spirit always begins His work of renewing the first love of Christians by bringing a conviction of sin on the part of the church. Carnal believers cannot wake up and begin right away in the service of God without deep searchings of heart. The fountains of sin need to be broken up. In a true revival, believers are always brought to see their sins in such a light that they often find it impossible to maintain a hope of their acceptance with God. It does not always go to this extent; but there are always, in genuine revival, deep convictions of sin, and often cases of abandoning all hope.

Carnal believers will be brought to repentance. A revival is simply a new beginning of obedience to God. And the first step is a deep repentance, a breaking down of the heart, a getting down into the dust before God, with deep humility, and forsaking sin.

Holy Spirit, I stand in great need of Your renewing my soul. Open my eyes to Your awesome display of love on Calvary, Lord Jesus. Expose my heart for what it really is like, no matter how ugly. Break me down in the dust that I might touch Your feet. Amen.

A Look into Our Heart

———⊰⊱———

*Brothers, my heart's desire
and prayer to God for the Israelites
is that they may be saved.*
—ROMANS 10:1

How can one determine whether he is a candidate for spiritual renewal? A look into the heart is a good beginning point. Here are characteristics I commonly find among believers:

Many believers are blind to the state of sinners. Their hearts are as hard as marble. The truths of the Bible only appear like a dream. They admit it to be all true; their conscience and their judgment assent to it; but their faith does not see it standing out in bold relief, in all the burning realities of eternity. But when they enter into a revival of spiritual power, they see men in a strong light that will renew the love of God in their hearts. This will lead them to labor zealously to bring others to Him, feeling grief that others do not love God as they do. And they will set themselves passionately to persuade their neighbors to give Him their hearts. So their love to men will be renewed. They will be filled with a tender, burning love for souls. They will be in an agony for individuals whom they want to have saved. They will not only be urging them to give their hearts to God, but they will carry them to God in the arms of faith, and with strong crying and tears beseech God to have mercy on them and save their souls from endless burnings.

> *Men act on their fellow men, not only by language but by their looks, their tears, their daily life.*

This is the work of the Holy Spirit. His power breaks the power of the world and of sin over believers. It brings believers to such vantage ground that they get a fresh impulse toward heaven. They have a new foretaste of heaven and new desires after union with God. The charm of the world is broken, and the power of sin overcome.

When a believer is thus awakened and reformed, the reformation and salvation of sinners will follow. Men act on their fellow men, not only by language but by their looks, their tears, their daily life. If a believer's life is full of worldliness, sinners read it. If a believer is full of the Spirit, sinners read it. The unbeliever who looks into the eyes of his godly wife sees the tenderness and compassion of the image of Christ, and her life is a constant sermon and reproach to him. He feels a sermon ringing in his ears all day long. Such is the power of the Spirit that leads others to a conviction of sin.

Father, the world sings its charming song wherever I go. Help me see through all the clutter and lies, and help me see the lives of people around me as You see them. Amen.

The Holy Spirit

———⦿———

"When he comes, he will convict
the world of guilt in regard to sin and
righteousness and judgment."
—JOHN 16:8

God's special agency is by His Holy Spirit. Having direct access to the mind, and knowing infinitely well every person, the Holy Spirit employs the truth that is best adapted to His particular case, and then sets it home with divine power. He gives it such a vividness, strength, and power, that the person quails, throws down his weapons of rebellion, and turns to the Lord. Under His influence, the truth burns and cuts its way like fire. He makes the truth stand out in such aspects that it crushes the proudest man down with the weight of a mountain. If men were disposed to obey God, the truth is given with sufficient clearness in the Bible that they could learn all that is necessary to know. But because they are wholly disinclined to obey it, God clears it up before their minds and pours in a blaze of convincing light upon their souls, which they cannot withstand, and they yield to it.

The Holy Spirit... enlightens our minds and makes the truth take hold of our souls.

In the same way, because we do not know what we should pray for as we should, the Holy Spirit makes intercession for the saints. He does not do it by praying for us while we do nothing. He prays for us by exciting our own faculties. Not that He suggests to us words or guides our language, but He enlightens our minds and makes the truth take hold of our souls. He leads us to consider the state of the church and the condition of sinners around us. The manner in which He brings the truth before the mind and keeps it there till it produces its effect, we cannot tell. But we can know this much—that He leads us to a deep consideration of the state of things; and the result of this, the natural and philosophical result, is deep feeling. That is, by turning away a man's thoughts, and leading him to think of other things. When the Holy Spirit brings a subject into warm contact with his heart, it is just as impossible he should not feel as it is that your hand should not feel a fire. If the Spirit of God leads a man to dwell on things calculated to excite warm and overpowering feelings, and he is not excited by them, it proves that he has no love for souls and knows nothing of the Spirit of Christ.

Holy Spirit, have Your divine way in my life. As You blazed the saving light of the gospel into my life, so enlighten my heart and mind that I might know Your voice today. You are God. Work Your will into my heart and life. Amen.

DAY 10

Revive Us

Will you not revive us again,
that your people may rejoice in you?
—PSALM 85:6

Psalm 85 seems to have been written soon after the return of the Jews from the Babylonian captivity. The psalmist felt that God had been very favorable to the people, and while considering the goodness of the Lord in restoring them to the land, he breaks out into a prayer for reviving of spiritual power among them. Such a petition should be the cry of our heart as well, especially when we see these sad signals:

When there is a lack of brotherly love among believers, then a revival of spiritual power is needed.

When believers are sunk down in carnality, they cannot possibly love in the same manner as when they are living holy lives. When Christ's image is not shining in them, or in other believers' lives, there is nothing in each other that produces this love. Indeed, the lack of love will open the door to dissension, jealousies, and evil speaking among believers. These things reflect how far believers are from God, and demand we call out for power from on high. Nothing can put an end to it except a visitation from God.

When there is a lack of brotherly love among believers, then a revival of spiritual power is needed.

When there is a worldly spirit in the church, it is manifested when you see believers conform to the world in dress, entertainment, and amusements. At such times the church will find its members falling into gross sins, giving the enemies of faith an occasion for reproach. Other members will become embroiled in controversies both within and outside of the church. Then it is that the wicked triumph over the church and revile believers. It is time for the church to ask of God, "What will become of Your great name?"

When sinners are careless and stupid, and sinking into hell unconcerned, it is time for believers to call out to God for spiritual power. It is as much the duty of the church to awake as it is of the firemen to awake when a fire breaks out in the night in a great city. The church ought to put out the fires of hell that are laying hold of the wicked. Sleep! Should the firemen sleep and let the whole city burn down, what would be thought of such firemen? And yet their guilt would not compare with the guilt of believers who sleep while sinners around them are sinking into the fires of hell.

———— ∞ ————

Father, I acknowledge that the fires of hell are burning in society around me, and even within the lives of church members. Revive me that my life may stand out as a light in the darkness. Wake me from my slumber, Lord, and put a fire in my soul. Amen.

A Tender Heart

⎯⎯⎯ ∞∞∞ ⎯⎯⎯

When the enemy shall come
in like a flood, the Spirit of the LORD
shall lift up a standard against him.
—ISAIAH 59:19 KJV

O ne clear indicator of spiritual power working in a believer's life is that the wickedness of the wicked grieves and humbles and distresses a believer. Sometimes believers do not seem to mind anything about the wicked around them. Or if they talk about it, it is in a cold, callous, and unfeeling way, as if they despaired of a reformation. They are disposed to scold at sinners, not to feel the compassion of the Son of God for them. But sometimes the conduct of the wicked drives believers to prayer, breaks them down, and makes them sorrowful and tender-hearted, so that they can weep day and night; and instead of scolding and reproaching them, they pray sincerely for them. Then you may expect power from on high. Indeed, this is a revival begun already in your heart.

If Christians are made to feel that they have no hope but in God…there will certainly be a revival.

Sometimes the wicked will get up an opposition to religion. And when this drives believers to their knees in prayer to God, with strong cryings and tears, you may be certain there is going to be a move of the Spirit. The prevalence and strength of wickedness is no evidence that there is not going to be revival. It is often God's time to work. If the devil is getting up something new in opposition to God working, it will either drive believers to God or farther away, deeper into carnality or something that will only make things worse. Frequently the most outrageous wickedness of the ungodly is followed by a revival. If Christians are made to feel that they have no hope but in God, and if they rise up to honor God and plead for the salvation of the souls of the unbelievers, there will certainly be a revival. Let hell boil over if it will, and spew out as many devils as there are stones in the pavements, if it only drives believers to God in prayer—hell cannot hinder the power of the Holy Spirit. Let Satan sound his horn as loud as he pleases; if Christians will only be humbled and pray, they shall soon see God's strong arm in a revival. I have known instances where a revival has broken in upon the enemy's ranks almost as suddenly as a clap of thunder and broken up their party in an instant.

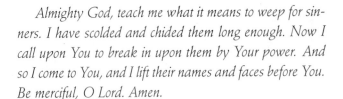

Almighty God, teach me what it means to weep for sinners. I have scolded and chided them long enough. Now I call upon You to break in upon them by Your power. And so I come to You, and I lift their names and faces before You. Be merciful, O Lord. Amen.

Full Surrender

———∞———

*"For we cannot help speaking about
what we have seen and heard."*
—ACTS 4:20

T he believers in the book of Acts showed a willingness to make any sacrifice necessary in order to receive the promised Holy Spirit and to carry on in His Spirit once they had received Him. This principle has never changed. Believers must be willing to sacrifice their feelings, their business, their time, to help forward the work. They must be willing to pursue Him with all their heart and strength. They must be willing to offend the impenitent by plain and faithful dealing in truth, and perhaps to offend church members who will not come up to the work. They must be willing to stand with the Spirit whatever the consequences may be, including being driven away from the church that resists the working of the Spirit. They must be determined to go straight forward and leave the rest with God.

And sacrifices will be involved. It will not do to say, "We desire to receive power from on high, but it cannot disturb our business practices or prevent us from making money." Believers must be willing

Believers must be willing to do anything, and sacrifice anything, that God indicates to be their duty

to do anything, and sacrifice anything, that God indicates to be their duty. I am not meaning that sacrifices be made to bribe God's favor, but if God calls individuals to specific sacrifices, one must be willing to do it.

One must also be willing to relinquish the control of how God pleases to pour out His spiritual power. Some believers try to prescribe to God what He shall direct and bless, and when and how. God will come in His own way, and one must never limit His working.

Do you desire the fullness of God's power working in your life through the Holy Spirit? If God should ask you this moment, by an audible voice from heaven, "Do you desire to be baptized with the Holy Spirit?" would you dare to say, Yes? When He asks, "Are you willing to make the sacrifices that I ask of you?" would you answer, let it begin at this moment—let it begin here—let it begin in my heart? Now? Would you dare to say so to God, if you heard His voice now?

———— ∞ ————

Jesus, Your disciples quickly discovered that the fullness of the Spirit led to imprisonment and possible death, but they readily spoke the truth as You gave them the words and power. Help me to sacrifice anything that prevents Your power from working in me. Amen.

Spiritual Feelings

———∞∞∞———

The eyes of all look to you, and you give them
their food at the proper time. You open your hand
and satisfy the desires of every living thing.
—PSALM 145:15–16

To receive power from on high, our minds must be prepared to receive the Holy Spirit, but people make great mistakes at this point by failing to understand the laws of the mind. People talk about spiritual feelings as if they thought they could, by direct effort, call forth spiritual affections for God. But this is not the way the mind works. No one can make himself feel in this way, merely by trying to feel. The feelings of the mind are not directly under our control. We cannot by willing, or by direct volition, call for spiritual feelings. We might as well try to call up spirits from the deep. Spiritual feelings are purely involuntary states of mind. They naturally and necessarily exist in the mind under certain circumstances calculated to excite them.

But spiritual affections can be controlled indirectly. Otherwise there would be no moral character in our feelings, if there were no way to control them. We cannot say, "Now I will feel so and so toward such an object." But we can command our attention to it, and look at it intently, till the involuntary affections arise. Let a man who is away from his family bring them up before his mind, and will he not feel? But it is not by saying to himself, "Now I will feel deeply for my family." A man can direct his attentions to any object, about which he ought to feel and wishes to feel, and in that way he will call into existence the proper emotions. Let a man call up his enemy before his mind, and his feelings of enmity will rise. So if a man thinks of God, and fastens his mind on any aspects of God's character, he will feel—emotions will come up, by

We cannot by willing, or by direct volition, call for spiritual feelings.

the very laws of mind. If he is a friend of God, let him contemplate God as a gracious and holy being, and he will have emotions of friendship kindled up in his mind. If he is an enemy of God, only let him get the true character of God before his mind, and look at it, and fasten his attention on it, and his enmity will rise against God, or he will break down and give his heart to God.

———⚬⚬⚬———

Heavenly Father, I have tried so hard to feel spiritual and to be spiritual, but it's never enough. I lift my eyes to You and see in You all that I could ever possibly need or want. Come to me, Holy Spirit, and fill me with the divine life. Amen.

Unplowed Hearts

*Break up your unplowed ground; for
it is time to seek the LORD, until he comes
and showers righteousness on you.*
—HOSEA 10:12

To break up the unplowed ground is to break up
your hearts—to prepare your minds to bring
forth fruit unto God. The mind of man is often compared in the Bible to soil, and the Word of God to
seed sown in it, and the fruit represents the actions
and affections of those who receive it. To break up
the mind, therefore, is to bring the mind into such a
state that it is ready to receive the Word of God.
Sometimes our heart gets matted down hard and
dry, and run to waste, till there is no such thing as

getting fruit from it until it is all broken up, mellowed down, and ready to receive the Word of God.

It is this softening of heart, so as to make it feel the truth, that the prophet Hosea calls breaking up your unplowed ground.

> *It is this softening of heart, so as to make it feel the truth, that the prophet Hosea calls breaking up your unplowed ground.*

Begin by looking at your heart—examine and note the state of your mind, and see where you are. Many believers pay no attention to their hearts and never know whether they are doing well spiritually or not—whether they are gaining or losing ground—whether they are fruitful or lying waste like fallow ground. Draw your attention away from other things and look into this. Do not be in a hurry. Examine whether you are walking with God every day, or walking with the devil—whether you are under the dominion of the prince of darkness, or of the Lord Jesus Christ.

Self-examination involves considering your actions, reviewing the past, and learning your true character.

Look back over your past history. Take up your individual sins one by one and look at them. I do not mean that you should just cast a glance at your past life and agree that it has been full of sins, and then go to God with a general confession and ask for forgiveness. You must take them up one by one. It will be a good thing to write them down, as you go over them, and allow your memory to bring them forth. General confession of sin will never do. Your sins were committed one by one; and as far as you can come at them, they should be reviewed and repented of one by one.

Father, I know how hardened my heart and mind can get. There are times when I read Your Word and listen for Your voice, but nothing can get in. Help me to break up the unplowed ground. My sins are before me. Help me to confess them honestly. Amen.

Sins of Omission

———∞∞∞———

*If we confess our sins, he is faithful
and just and will forgive us our sins and
purify us from all unrighteousness.*
—1 JOHN 1:9

Sin bars the door to the fullness of the Holy Spirit. Open your heart and let Him expose anything that may be there that prevents Him from working in your life.

Ingratitude. Write down all the instances you can remember when you have received favors from God, for which you have never exercised gratitude. How many cases can you remember? Some remarkable providence, some wonderful turn of events, that saved you from ruin. The numerous mercies you have received with a half-thankful heart. Or other instances when your ingratitude is so black that you are forced to hide your face in shame! Go to your knees and confess them one by one to God, and ask forgiveness.

Have you not given your heart to other loves and infinitely offended Him?

Lack of love to God. Consider all the times when you have not given the blessed God the hearty love that you should have. Think how grieved and alarmed you would be if you discovered that due to your lack of love for your spouse that another person had engrossed their heart and thoughts. Now, God tells us He is a jealous God, and have you not given your heart to other loves and infinitely offended Him?

Neglect of the Bible. Put down the cases when for days, or weeks, you had no pleasure in God's Word. Perhaps you did read it, but with so little attention that you cannot remember where or what your read. You read it as a task rather than from love for the Word of God. The Word is the rule of your duty. And do you pay so little regard to it?

Unbelief. Instances where you have virtually charged the God of truth with lying, by your unbelief of His express promises and declarations. God had promised to give the Holy Spirit to those who ask Him. Now, have you believed this? Have you expected Him to answer? Have you not rather virtually said in your heart, "I do not believe that I shall receive Him?" Is this not to charge God with lying?

Neglect of prayer. Times when you have neglected prayer, or have prayed in such a way as more grievously to offend God than to have neglected it altogether.

Holy Spirit, my sins are so ugly that I hate to consider them. But I know how they cut me off from Your fullness and power and love. I confess them to You, one by one. Break the power that they have over my life. Free me to love Jesus with all my heart. Amen.

Sins of Commission

———— ∞∞∞ ————

He who conceals his sins does not
prosper, but whoever confesses and
renounces them finds mercy.
—PROVERBS 28:13

Worldliness. How have you regarded your worldly possessions? Have you looked at them as really yours—as if you had a right to dispose of them as your own, according to your own will? If you have, write it down. If you have loved property, and sought after it for its own sake, or to gratify lust and ambition or a worldly spirit, you have sinned.

Pride. How many times have you thought more and taken more pains about decorating your body to go to church than you have about preparing your mind for the worship of God? Cared more about pleasing others than in how your soul appears in the sight of the heart-searching God?

Envy. Look at the times when you were envious of those whom you thought were above you in any respect or more talented or useful than you. Have you not so envied some that you were pained to hear them praised? You chose rather to dwell upon their faults than upon their virtues.

> *Have you not so envied some that you were pained to hear them praised?*

Evil speaking and slander. Instances when you have had a bitter spirit and spoke of believers in a manner entirely devoid of love and charity. Times when you have spoken behind others' backs of their faults, real or supposed, of members of the church or others, unnecessarily or without good reason. You need not lie to be guilty of slander; to tell the truth with the design to injure is slander.

Lying. Any species of designed deception for a selfish reason is lying. If you design to make an impression—by words or looks or actions—contrary to the naked truth, God calls it a lie and charges you with lying.

Cheating. Write down whenever you have dealt with a person and done to him that which you would not like him to have done to you. That is cheating.

Hypocrisy. For instance, how many times have you confessed sins that you did not mean to break off? Or prayed to impress others rather than God?

Robbing God. Instances when you have misspent your time and squandered hours that God gave you to serve Him. Times when you have misapplied your abilities or wasted your money on things you did not need.

Father, bring to my mind any sin that I have tried to hide or forget about. Help me to truly repent, to confess and renounce it. I want Your mercy and the fullness of Your Spirit to flow into my life and through my life to others. May Jesus be glorified. Amen.

Drive the Plow Deep

———⸎———

Wash away all my iniquity
and cleanse me from my sin.
—PSALM 51:2

In breaking up your unplowed ground, you must remove every obstruction. Don't put it off; that will only make the matter worse. Confess to God those sins that have been committed against God, and to man those sins that have been committed against man. Don't think of getting off by going around the stumbling block. Take them up out of the way. Things may be left that you may think little things, and you may wonder why you have not broken through to God, when the reason is that

55

your proud and carnal mind has covered up something that God has put His finger on. Break up all
the ground and turn it over. Do not balk at it, as the
farmers say; do not turn aside for lit-
tle difficulties; drive the plow right
through them, beam deep, and turn
the ground all up, so that it may all be
mellow and soft and ready to receive
the seed and bear fruit a hundredfold.

Whenever you find anything wrong, resolve at once, in the strength of God, to sin no more in that way.

When you have gone over your
whole history, then go over the
ground a second time just as carefully.
You will find that the things you have
put down will suggest other things of
which you have been guilty, con-
nected with or near them. Unless you
consider them in detail, one by one, you can form
no idea of the amount of your sins. Go over it as
carefully as you would if you were preparing to
stand before God's judgment.

As you go over the catalog of your sins, be sure to
resolve upon present and entire reformation. Whenever you find anything wrong, resolve at once, in the

strength of God, to sin no more in that way. It will be of no benefit to examine yourself, unless you determine to amend in every particular that you find wrong in heart, attitude, and conduct.

You never will have the Spirit of God dwelling in you until you have unraveled this whole mystery of iniquity and set your sins before God. If after searching your heart your mind is still dark, look again and you will find there is some reason for the Spirit of God to not come to you. With the Bible before you, try your heart until you do feel the weight and darkness of your sin. Let there be this deep work of repentance, and full confession, this breaking down before God, and surely He will come.

Gracious Father, in the light of Your Word, I ask You to get to the very depths of my heart. Root out even the little things that I have glossed over and pretended didn't matter. Cleanse my soul of all that withholds Your light and glory. Amen.

A Prepared Heart

—◦◦◦—

*"Wake up, O sleeper, rise from the dead,
and Christ will shine on you."*
—EPHESIANS 5:14

It will do no good to speak of spiritual power while your heart is in a hardened, waste, and unplowed state. The farmer might just as well sow his grain on the rock. It will bring forth no fruit. This is the reason why there are so many fruitless believers in the church, and why there is so little deep-toned feeling in the church. Look at the Sunday school for instance, and see how much potential there is, and how little of the power of godliness. If you go on in this way, the Word of God will continue to harden you, and you will grow worse and worse, just as the rain and snow on an unplowed field makes the turf thicker and harder.

See why so much preaching and teaching is wasted, and worse than wasted: it is because the church will not break up their fallow ground. A preacher may wear out his life, and do very little good, while there are many stony-grounded hearers, who have never had their unplowed hearts broken up. There is mechanical religion enough, but very little that looks like deep heart-work.

Will you enter upon the course now pointed out, and persevere until you are thoroughly awake?

Believers must never satisfy themselves, or expect spiritual power, just by waking up, and blustering about, and making a noise, and talking to sinners. They must get their fallow ground broken up. It is utterly unphilosophical to think of getting engaged in religion in this way. If your fallow ground is broken up, then the way to get more feeling is to go out and see sinners on the road to hell, and talk to them, and guide inquiring souls, and you will get more feeling. You may get into an excitement without this breaking up; you may show a kind of zeal, but it will not last long, and it will not take hold of sinners, unless your heart is broken up. The reason is that you go about it mechanically and have not plowed your hard heart.

Will you enter upon the course now pointed out, and persevere until you are thoroughly awake? If you fail here, if you do not get your heart prepared, you can go no further with the Holy Spirit. Any more said about it will only harden and make you worse.

Father, it's scary to think that when our hearts are unbroken, even Your Word will increase our hardness when we refuse to hear it. Holy Spirit, awaken my heart in every sense and breathe Your life into my soul. May You do a deep heart-work in me. Amen.

Prevailing Prayer

———— ∞∞∞ ————

*The prayer of a righteous man
is powerful and effective.*
—JAMES 5:16

There are two kinds of means requisite to the reception of spiritual power; one to influence men, and the other to influence God. The truth is employed to influence men, and prayer to move God. When I speak of moving God, I do not mean that God's mind is changed by prayer, or that His character or attitude is changed. But prayer produces such a change *in us* and fulfills such conditions as renders it consistent for God to do as it would not be consistent for Him to do otherwise. When a sinner repents, that state of mind makes it proper for God to forgive him. God has always been ready to forgive him on that condition, so that when the sinner changes his mind toward God, it requires no change of feeling in God to pardon him. So when believers offer effectual prayer, their state of mind renders it proper for God to answer them. He was always ready to bestow the blessing of the Holy Spirit, on the condition that they felt right and offered the right kind of prayer.

When believers offer effectual prayer, their state of mind renders it proper for God to answer them.

Prayer is an essential link in the chain of causes that lead to spiritual power; as much so as truth is. Prevailing prayer is that prayer that obtains the blessing it seeks, that effectually moves God. Some have zealously sought the truth but laid very little stress on prayer, and then wondered that they had so little success. They overlook the fact that truth by itself will never produce the effect, without the Spirit of God, and that the Spirit is given in answer to earnest prayer.

Sometimes it happens that those who are the most engaged in employing truth are not the most engaged in prayer. This is always unhappy, for unless they have the spirit of prayer, the truth by itself will do nothing but harden men in impenitence. Others err on the opposite side. Not that they lay too much stress on prayer. But they overlook the fact that prayer might be offered forever, by itself, and nothing would be done. God always works by the power of the Holy Spirit through the truth of His Word. To expect the Spirit to work without the employment of the truth is to tempt God.

Lord Jesus, if anyone ever persevered in prayer, it was You. Come to my side, with Your truth and Spirit, and teach me what it means to pray. Reshape my life through prayer, and open the door to power from on high as You did on the day of Pentecost. Amen.

Perseverance in Prayer

———— ✖ ————

Then Jesus told his disciples
a parable to show them that they should
always pray and not give up.
—LUKE 18:1

When a person prays for a specific desire, such as the baptism of the Holy Spirit, it must be a persevering prayer. Far too many believers are not prepared in heart, and they cannot fix their minds and hold on till the blessing comes. They have to pray again and again, because their thoughts are so apt to wander to something else. Until their minds get imbued with the spirit of prayer, they will not keep fixed to one point and push their petition to an issue on the spot. Do not think you are prepared to offer prevailing prayer if your feelings will let you pray once for an object and then leave it. Most believers come up to prevailing prayer by a protracted process. Their minds gradually become filled with such concern that they go about their business sighing out their desires to God.

What was the reason that Jacob wrestled all night in prayer with God? He knew that his brother Esau was on the way to meet him with an armed force,

Do not think you are prepared to offer prevailing prayer if your feelings will let you pray once for an object and then leave it.

and there was great reason to suppose Esau was coming to revenge Jacob's past wrongs. So, he first arranges everything in the best manner he can to meet his brother, sending his present first, then his property, and finally his family farthest behind. By this time his mind was so exercised that he could not contain himself. He goes away alone over the brook and pours out his soul in an agony of prayer all night. And just at daybreak, the angel of the covenant said, "Let me go." Jacob's whole being was, as it were, agonized at the thought of giving up, and he cried out, "I will not let you go unless you bless me" (Gen. 32:26). His soul was worked up into an agony, and he obtained the blessing. This is prevailing prayer.

Do not deceive yourself into thinking that you offer effectual prayer unless you have this intense desire for the blessing. Prayer is not effectual unless it is offered with an agony of desire. The apostle Paul spoke of it as a travail of the soul. Jesus Christ, when He prayed in the Garden, was in such an agony that he sweat great drops of blood. I have known persons to pray till their strength was all exhausted. Such prayers prevailed with God.

Almighty Father, I cannot bear fruit and bring glory to Your Son apart from the fullness of the Holy Spirit. I will not rest, I will not give up, I will call on Your name until You hear from heaven and do this work in my life. Do it now, for Jesus' sake. Amen.

Holy Violence

———— ❧ ————

*But Jacob replied, "I will not let
you go unless you bless me."*
—GENESIS 32:26

E ffectual prayer for the fullness of the Holy Spirit
implies a desire that bears some proportion to
the greatness of the blessing. If a person truly desires
any blessing, something not contrary to the will and
providence of God, the presumption is that it will be
granted.

If the Holy Spirit is stirring your desires for His
presence, no degree of desire or importunity in prayer
is improper. A believer may come up, as it were, and
take hold of the hand of God. Was God displeased

with Jacob's boldness and importunity when he exclaimed that he would not let the angel of the covenant go without a blessing? Not at all, but God granted him the very thing he prayed for. So in the case of Moses. God said to Moses, "I will strike them down with a plague and destroy them, but I will make you into a nation greater and stronger than they" (Num. 14:12). What did Moses do? Did he stand aside and let God do as He said? No, his mind ran back to the Egyptians, and he declared, "Then the Egyptians will hear about it!" (vs. 13). It seemed as if he took hold of the uplifted hand of God to avert the blow. Did God rebuke him for this interference and tell him he had no business to intercede? No, it seemed as if he was unable to deny anything to such importunity, and so Moses stood in the gap and prevailed with God.

A believer may come up, as it were, and take hold of the hand of God.

It is said of the missionary Xavier that he was once called to pray for a man who was sick, and he prayed so fervently that he seemed to do violence to heaven—so the writer expressed it. And Xavier prevailed, and the man recovered.

Such prayer is often offered in the present day, when believers have been wrought upon to such a pitch of importunity and such a holy boldness that afterward, when they looked back upon it, they were frightened and amazed at themselves, to think they should dare to exercise such importunity with God. And yet these persons are among the holiest people I know in the world.

Holy Spirit, I know that Pentecost was a day of great delight to our Father. May the same be true today. Reign in my life and bring resounding praise to Jesus. Grip my heart and soul with truth, and may Jesus be exalted in everything I do and say. Amen.

God's Promise

———∞∞∞———

"Therefore I tell you, whatever you
ask for in prayer, believe that you have
received it, and it will be yours.
—MARK 11:24

That faith is an indispensable condition of prevailing prayer is undoubtable. I am speaking
now of the kind of faith that *secures* the blessing. We
are to believe that we shall receive a specific thing
we ask for. We are not to think that God is such a
being that if we ask a fish, He will give us a serpent,
or if we ask bread, He will give us a stone. In Mark
11 the disciples were to have faith for a miracle, and
it is plain that they were bound to believe they
should receive the very thing itself. That is what

they were to believe. Now what should men believe in regard to other blessings? Is it a mere loose idea that if a man prays for a specific blessing, God will by some mysterious sovereignty give something or other to him, or something to somebody else, somewhere? Such a thought is utter nonsense and highly dishonorable to God. No, we are to believe that we shall receive the very things we ask for.

> *We are to believe that we shall receive the very things we ask for.*

When are we bound to make this prayer? When are we bound to believe that we shall have the very things we pray for? I answer, when we have evidence for it. Faith must always have evidence. A man cannot believe a thing unless he sees something that he supposes to be evidence. He is under no obligation to believe, and has no right to believe, a thing will be done unless he has evidence. It is the height of fanaticism to believe without evidence.

Suppose that God has especially promised the thing. For instance, God says He is more ready to give His Holy Spirit to those who ask Him than parents are to give bread to their children. Here we are bound to believe that we shall receive it when we pray for it. You have no right to put in an *if* and say, "Lord, *if it is Your will,* give me Your Holy Spirit." This is to insult God. To put an *if* into God's promise, where God has put none, is tantamount to charging God with being insincere. It is like saying, "O God, if You are sincere in making this promise, grant the blessing I have prayed for."

———— ✺ ————

Heavenly Father, my earthly father never gave me a serpent when I desired bread, and I believe that You are more than willing and able to give me the gift of the Holy Spirit. I thank You for Your grace, for I surely don't deserve the fullness of His presence. Amen.

Selfish Prayers

———— ∞ ————

In the same way, the Spirit helps us in
our weakness. We do not know what we ought
to pray for, but the Spirit himself intercedes for us
with groans that words cannot express.
—ROMANS 8:26

How shall we get this influence of the Spirit of God in our lives? It must be sought by fervent, believing prayer.

The Father has said He delights to give the Holy Spirit to those who ask Him. Does anyone say, I have prayed for Him, and He does not come? It is "because you ask with wrong motives, that you may spend what you get on your pleasures" (James 4:3). A prominent believer in a church once told his minister that he had been praying for weeks for the

Spirit and had not received Him. The minister asked the man what his motive was in praying. The reply was that he wanted to be happy like others he knew who had the Spirit. The minister replied that the devil himself might pray this way. It is mere selfishness. The man turned away in anger, convinced he was a hypocrite and that his prayers were all selfish. In contrast, David prayed that God would uphold him by His free Spirit that he might teach transgressors and turn sinners to God (Ps. 51:13). A believer should pray for the Spirit that he may be the more useful and glorify God more, not that he might be more happy. We need to examine ourselves and see if all our prayers are not selfish.

> *A believer should pray for the Spirit that he may be the more useful and glorify God more, not that he might be more happy.*

Use the means adapted to stir up your mind on the subject and keep your attention focused there. If a man prays for the Spirit, and then diverts his mind to other objects; uses no other means, but goes right away to worldly objects; he tempts God, he swings loose from his object, and it would be a miracle if he should get what he prays for. God is not going to pour this blessing on you without any effort of your own. You must cherish the slightest impressions of His Spirit. Take the Bible and go over the passages that show the condition and prospect of the world. Look at the world, look at your neighbors and children, and see their condition while they remain in sin. Then you will persevere in prayer and effort till you obtain the blessing of the Spirit of God to dwell in you.

Holy Spirit, selfishness has tainted every part of my life, including my prayers, and even my desire for what is obviously Your will for me. Work in my heart until my motives are purified from the desire for happiness or pride. May You be the reason for it all. Amen.

Holy Discipleship

———— ∞ ————

Be filled with the Spirit.
—EPHESIANS 5:18

What are the consequences of having the Spirit of God working in power in your life? You will be called eccentric, and probably you will deserve it. I never knew a person who was filled with the Spirit who was not called eccentric. And the reason is that they are unlike other people. They act under different influences, take different views, are moved by different motives, are led by a different spirit. There is such a thing as being so deeply imbued with the Spirit of God that you must and will act so as to appear strange and eccentric to those who do not understand your conduct. The apostle Paul was accused of being insane by those who did not understand why he acted as he did (Acts 26:24). But the truth was that Paul only saw the subject so clearly that he threw his whole soul into it. To walk with God and live above the standards of the world will put you at odds with it.

If you have the Spirit of God, you must expect to feel great distress in view of the church and the world. Some believers ask for the Spirit because they think it will make them so perfectly happy. There never was a greater mistake. Read your Bible and note how the prophets and apostles were always groaning and distressed in view of the state of the church and the world. The apostle Paul said he was always bearing about in his body the dying of the Lord Jesus (2 Cor. 4:10–12). The more you have of His Spirit, the more clearly you will see the state of sinners and believers, and the more deeply

> *To walk with God and live above the standards of the world will put you at odds with it.*

you will be distressed about them. Many times your distress will be unutterable (Rom. 9:1–3).

And you will be often grieved with the state of the ministry. Spiritual believers often weep and groan in secret when they see the darkness on the minds of their ministers in regard to the Spirit, their worldliness, and fear of man. The spirituality of the ministry, though real, is often so superficial that the pastor cannot and does not sympathize with those who are spiritual. The preaching does not meet their needs, does not feed them, does not meet their experience. Though he may preach sound doctrine, he remains in spiritual babyhood and needs to be fed rather than undertake the feeding of the church.

Father, I know that to follow Jesus involves a calling that sets me apart from the world. Fill me with the Holy Spirit that I might make an impact on the lives of those around me. I count it my greatest privilege to be called Your child. Amen.

Opposition

———❦———

In fact, everyone who wants to live a godly
life in Christ Jesus will be persecuted.
—2 TIMOTHY 3:12

I f you have much of the Spirit of God, you must
be prepared to have much opposition both in the
church and the world. It is likely that leaders in the
church will oppose you. There has always been
opposition in the church. So it was when Christ was
on earth. I see spiritual believers often ostracized and
opposed by church elders and even ministers.

You must expect very frequent and agonizing
conflicts with Satan. Satan has very little trouble with
believers who are lukewarm and carnal-minded, who

do not understand what is said about spiritual conflicts. They smile when such things are mentioned,
and so the devil lets them alone. They don't disturb
him, nor he them. But Satan under-
stands that spiritual Christians are
doing him a vast injury, and, therefore, he sets himself against them.
Spiritual believers often have terrible
conflicts. They have temptations they
never thought of before, blasphemous
thoughts, suggestions to do deeds of
wickedness, to destroy their own
lives, and the like. If you are spiritual,
you may expect these conflicts.

> *Satan understands that spiritual Christians are doing him a vast injury, and, therefore, he sets himself against them.*

You will have greater conflicts
within yourself. You will sometimes
find your own corruptions making
strange headway against the Spirit. "The flesh lusteth
against the Spirit, and the Spirit against the flesh"
(Gal. 5:17 KJV). I have known spiritual believers to
groan a great part of the night in conflict with inner
corruption, crying to God in agony that the power of
the temptation will be broken.

But you will have peace with God. If the church, and sinners, and the devil oppose you, there will be One with whom you have peace. Let those of you who are called to these trials, conflicts, and temptations, and who groan, pray, weep, and break your hearts, remember this consideration: your peace, so far as your feelings toward God are concerned, will flow like a river. And you will have peace of conscience if you are led by the Spirit. You will not be constantly goaded and kept on the rack by a guilty conscience. Your conscience will be calm and quiet, unruffled as the summer's lake.

—⊗—

Father, I am not afraid to face opposition, whether from the devil or from others, as long as I know that I am in the center of Your will. May the peace of Your Holy Spirit reign over my heart and life, no matter what I face. Amen.

Peace or Power

---oeoo---

*"'Not by might nor by power, but by my
Spirit,' says the LORD Almighty."*
—ZECHARIAH 4:6

There is a great difference between the *peace* and the *power* of the Holy Spirit in the soul. The disciples were Christians before the Day of Pentecost, and, as such, had a measure of the Holy Spirit. They must have had the peace of sins forgiven, and of a justified state, but yet they had not the endowment of power necessary to the accomplishment of the work assigned them. They had the peace that Christ had given them, but not the power that He had promised. This may be true of all believers, and right here is, I think, the great mistake of the church and of the ministry. They rest in conversion and do not seek until they have obtained power from on high. Hence so many believers have no power with either God or man. They prevail with neither. They cling to a hope in Christ, and even enter the ministry, overlooking the admonition to wait until they have been baptized with the Holy Spirit.

They had the peace that Christ had given them, but not the power that He had promised.

Why is this so when Christ has promised the Spirit to those who ask? Why so much prayer offered and yet so few believers who have received power from on high? Why the great gulf between the asking and receiving?

My answer is that we are not willing, upon the whole, to have what we desire and ask. God has expressly informed us that if we regard iniquity in our hearts He will not hear us. If we are self-indulgent, uncharitable, censorious, self-dependent, resistant to conviction of sin, refusing to confess our sin to those we have offended or need to make restitution toward, what do we expect? If we are prejudiced and uncandid, revengeful, dishonest, caught up in worldly ambitions, we grieve away the Spirit. We quench the Spirit by persistence in justifying wrong, neglecting prayer and study of His Word, resisting His teachings, and refusing to consecrate ourselves entirely to God. Last and greatest, by our unbelief we insult God by refusing to expect to receive what He has promised. What a blasphemy to accuse God of lying!

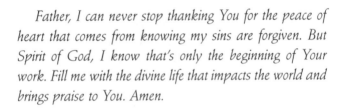

Father, I can never stop thanking You for the peace of heart that comes from knowing my sins are forgiven. But Spirit of God, I know that's only the beginning of Your work. Fill me with the divine life that impacts the world and brings praise to You. Amen.

DAY 27

Innocent Amusements

So whether you eat or drink or whatever
you do, do it all for the glory of God.
—1 CORINTHIANS 10:31

I hear much said of indulging in innocent amusements. In light of Paul's words, it is plain that it is
not innocent to engage in amusements merely to gratify the desire for amusement. God has made eating
and drinking pleasant to us, but this pleasure is not
to be our ultimate reason for indulging in it. We are
bound to have a higher motive than self-gratification.
God has not said, "Seek whatever you want because
you want it," but to do all from love to God and
man. No amusement is innocent unless the ultimate

motive is to please and honor God. To be innocent, an amusement must be engaged in because it is believed to be pleasing to God, as honoring Him more than anything else that we can engage in for the time being. Anything less will result in a depletion of spiritual power.

> *No amusement is innocent unless the ultimate motive is to please and honor God.*

No amusement can be innocent that involves the squandering of time and money that might be better employed to the glory of God and the good of man. Life is short. Time is precious. We live in a fallen world in desperate need of spiritual light. We are required to work while the day lasts. All our time and money are the Lord's. We are the Lord's. The loose manner in which this subject is viewed is surprising and alarming.

Right here is the delusion of many believers, I fear. When speaking of amusements, they say, "What harm is there in them?" On the surface they see nothing contrary to morality, and therefore judge it as innocent. They fail to ask whether the act is actually done with a single eye to God's glory and kingdom. No act or course of action should be counted as innocent without ascertaining the supreme motive of the person who acts.

So are we never to seek such amusements? I say that it is our privilege and duty to live above a desire for such things. Every desire should be subdued by living in the light of God and communion with the Spirit as not to feel the necessity of such amusements to make his enjoyment satisfactory. The highest and purest of all amusements is found in doing the will of God.

Lord Jesus, I live in a world that is consumed with the pursuit of pleasure. Draw me into the secret place of Your presence, and may my delights be discovered in You. Holy Spirit, I can never cut through the clutter unless You work powerfully in my life. Amen.

Pleasure Seeking

———∞∞∞———

And whatever you do, whether in word or deed,
do it all in the name of the Lord Jesus, giving
thanks to God the Father through him.
—COLOSSIANS 3:17

I s this word from the apostle Paul to be taken as a yoke of bondage? I am not surprised that it creates in some minds a real disturbance. The pleasure-loving and pleasure-seeking members of the church regard it as impractical, as a straitjacket, as a bondage. But surely it is not to anyone who loves God with all his heart and his neighbor as himself. Their own interests and pleasures are regarded as nothing as compared with the interests and good pleasure of God. They find their highest happiness in pleasing the One they love supremely and seeking the good of their fellow men. Jesus Christ said that His yoke is easy and His burden is light. The requirement to do all for the glory of God is surely none other than the yoke of Christ. It is His expressed will. It is not hard or heavy to a willing, loving mind.

Surely a believer must be fallen from his first love of Jesus if he must turn back to the world for satisfaction. A spiritual mind cannot find enjoyment in worldly society. To such a mind that society is necessarily repulsive. Worldly society is insincere, hollow, and to a great extent a sham. To a mind in communion with God, their worldly spirit and ways are repulsive and painful, as it is strongly suggestive of the downward tendency of their souls and the destiny that awaits them. It is the privilege of every believer to rise, through grace, above a hungering and thirsting for the fleshpots of Egypt, worldly pastimes, and time-wasting amusements.

> *The requirement to do all for the glory of God is surely none other than the yoke of Christ.*

Believers who desire to live in the fullness of the Spirit are bound to maintain a life consistent with their calling. We must deny worldly lusts and abstain from all outward manifestation of such inward lustings. We are to live above the world, as consisting with a heavenly mind that affords an enjoyment so spiritual and heavenly as to render the low pursuits and joys of worldly men disagreeable and repulsive. It is a sad stumbling block to the unconverted to see believers seeking happiness from this world.

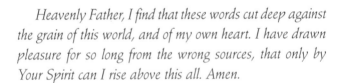

Heavenly Father, I find that these words cut deep against the grain of this world, and of my own heart. I have drawn pleasure for so long from the wrong sources, that only by Your Spirit can I rise above this all. Amen.

Spiritual Growth

———— ✑✑ ————

But grow in the grace and knowledge
of our Lord and Savior Jesus Christ.
—2 PETER 3:18

A condition of growth in grace and spiritual power is an intense earnestness and constancy in seeking increased religious light by the illumination of the Holy Spirit. You will gain no effectual spiritual light except by the inward showing and teaching of the Holy Spirit. This you will not obtain unless you continue in the attitude of a disciple of Christ. Remember, He says, "Any of you who does not give up everything he has cannot be my disciple" (Luke 14:33). He will not, by His Holy Spirit, be your divine teacher unless you renounce self and live in a state of continual consecration to Him. To obtain and preserve the teachings of Christ, by His Holy Spirit, you must continually and earnestly pray for His divine teaching, and watch against resisting and grieving Him.

Every step in the Christian life is to be taken under the influence of the Holy Spirit.

Another condition of growth in grace is constant conformity to all the teachings of the Holy Spirit, keeping up with our convictions of duty and with our growing knowledge of the will of God.

A greater and more all-pervading fullness of the Holy Spirit's residence is another condition of growth in the favor of God. You cannot have it too thoroughly impressed upon you that every step in the Christian life is to be taken under the influence of the Holy Spirit. The thing to be attained is the universal teaching and guidance of the Holy Spirit, so that in *all* things you shall be led by the Spirit of God. "So I say, live by the Spirit, and you will not gratify the desires of the sinful nature" (Gal. 5:16).

"For if you live according to the sinful nature, you will die; but if by the Spirit you put to death the misdeeds of the body, you will live" (Rom. 8:13). "The mind of sinful man is death, but the mind controlled by the Spirit is life and peace" (Rom. 8:6). Always remember, therefore, that to grow in grace, you must grow in the possession of the fullness of the Holy Spirit in your heart.

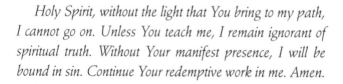

Holy Spirit, without the light that You bring to my path, I cannot go on. Unless You teach me, I remain ignorant of spiritual truth. Without Your manifest presence, I will be bound in sin. Continue Your redemptive work in me. Amen.

Fresh Anointings

———◦◦◦———

After they prayed, the place where
they were meeting was shaken. And they
were all filled with the Holy Spirit and
spoke the word of God boldly. ·
—ACTS 4:31

Remember that every step of progress in the
Christian life must be made by faith, and not
by works. The mistake that many good men make
on this point is truly amazing. Indeed, the custom
has become almost universal to represent growth in
grace as consisting in the formation of habits of obedience to God.

The fact is that every step of progress in the Christian life is taken by a fresh and fuller appropriation
of Christ by faith, a fuller baptism of the Holy Spirit.

As our weaknesses, infirmities, besetting sins, and necessities are revealed to us by the circumstances of temptation through which we pass, our only efficient help is found in Christ, and we grow only as we step by step more fully appropriate Him, in one relation or another, and more fully "clothe yourselves with the Lord Jesus Christ" (Rom. 13:14). As we are more and more emptied of self-dependence, as we more and more renounce and discard all expectation of forming holy habits by any obedience of ours, and as by faith we secure deeper and deeper baptisms of the Holy Spirit, and put on the Lord Jesus Christ more and more thoroughly and in more of His official relations, by just so much the faster do we grow in the favor of God.

Nothing can be more erroneous and dangerous than the commonly received idea of growing in grace by the formation of holy habits.

Nothing can be more erroneous and dangerous than the commonly received idea of growing in grace by the formation of holy habits. By acts of faith alone through the Holy Spirit we appropriate Christ, and we are as truly sanctified by faith as we are justified by faith. You must pray in faith for the Holy Spirit. You must appropriate and put on Christ through the Holy Spirit. At every forward step in your progress you must have a fresh anointing of the Holy Spirit through faith.

———— ⚬⚭⚬ ————

Heavenly Father, may my faith always be wielded to You. Lead me into deeper and deeper baptisms of Your Spirit that I might glorify Jesus through all of my life. May I love and serve You forever. Amen.